The Mentor's Resource Manual

PREPARED FOR:

PROJECT TRANSFORMATION

Peter S. Pierro, Ed.D.

Prepared for Publication by:

www.40DayPublishing.com

Published by:

www.WideAwakeBooks.com

Printed in the United States of America

Dedication

This book is dedicated to our children who learn to read so that they may learn about the Arts, History, Literature, Mathematics, Science, and most important, about Themselves.

Acknowledgements

My thanks to all of the great teachers I have taught with - who have enriched my life as well as making me a better teacher and a better person.

A special thanks to Doug Johnston for helping me stay focused during this production. I would have loved to have had him as a fellow teacher during our earlier careers.

A special thank you to Cathi Nelson; a master teacher, tennis coach, tutor, and advisor. She was especially helpful when I was dealing with caring, bonding issues.

A very special appreciation for that gifted musician, loving and caring teacher, companion, and wife, Bobbie Bullard Pierro (1934-2017).

Contents

Prologue

What am I doing here?
What do I do and how do I do it?

A few years ago I decided to join three of my retired friends in a child mentoring program. I have had several different mentoring experiences. One was with a small group of 3rd graders for half a school year in a local public school. This mentoring had been a difficult one for me because it had to do entirely with giving these children practice for doing well on the upcoming achievement tests. The material consisted entirely of having the children read stories similar to those in reading workbooks and then having them respond to a list of fact-recall, multiple choice items instead of the usual discussion questions. Also I have been involved in many mentoring experiences with individual elementary age students and adults who were having reading difficulties.

Now, I was sitting at a table in a church basement waiting for my first session with Maria, a 2nd grade child. We mentors had had a two hour orientation the week before that was based on the operational aspects of the mentoring program and included a short get acquainted meeting at the cooperating school with Maria's teacher and mother. There had been no mention of a reading assistance program being used with our children

I had been told by my friends that the mentoring had to do basically with reading. Was I supposed to follow a program that was in synch with her reading instruction in school? Was she going to bring in her reading home-work and have me help her? Or was I to just listen to her read to me and have a discussion about what she had read? Were we to play some of those phonics games on the shelves? How about going through some of those flash cards at her grade level? Was I going to get any more guidelines and information as the year progressed?

I soon realized that we were not going to be given any more guidelines or information in dealing with the reading skills of our children. Since I felt that I was given latitude in what to do and how to do it, I decided to use the methods in *Growing and Learning*, the book I had written on how young children learn to read. This program is described in this book in the section on The Infant Child School. Using this approach the entire year went very well for both me and Maria. Subsequently, I went on to mentor children at a higher level – 4th and 5th graders. My operation with these kids was a little different and is described in the section on The Junior School. There is one saying in education on reading that makes good sense if we interpret in with the belief that there are individual differences among our children;

In Grades One to Three, the Child learns to read.

In Grades Four and after, the Child reads to learn.

The Problem

My operation worked out well for me but I got a different insight into what was happening with other mentors, new and experienced. I had befriended George, another new mentor, during the orientation session and he spent a lot of time with me asking what to do and how to do it. It became evident to me that people who had no training or experience in teaching children had to be having problems. "What do I do and how do I do it?" sums up the concern of George and other mentors.

One other area of concern was about teaching their kids about phonics. They heard children being told "When two vowels go walking, the first does the talking" and the children seemed to know what that means. What it means to me is that, in and of itself, it's pretty poor advice since it is correct in only 36% of our 2000 most commonly used words. (There is much more on this in the section on Phonics.)

The greatest contribution mentors, and it's a big one, is that the children find another adult who cares about them and is interested in what they are doing. However, if we expect there to be some improvement in the reading abilities of our learners, mentors need guidance and direction of some kind. We can't expect people who have had no teaching experience or instruction in teaching reading to children to do more than read to them and to listen to them read. Even the use of flash cards is done poorly without instruction.

The Proposal

Two very simple reading instruction programs were developed in England during the time of World War II. They were the basis for the education of many of our children during the period from the 1950s to the 1980s, now commonly called The Golden Age of Education. In England, they were called The British Infant School and The Junior School. In the United States, we called it Progressive Education, The Open Classroom, and Individualized Learning. *

Our mentors can join the uneducated and untrained mentors in England in the 1940s who gave their children excellent reading learning experiences. As indicated above, the British Infant and Junior Schools are presented in upcoming chapters.

* If you're curious, in the 1980s and up to now, all of this has been replaced by the Achievement Testing movement.

The Task of the Mentor – Creating a Learning Environment

Just Being There is the Most Important Factor

There isn't a lot of research about the effects of outside school mentoring on children's performance on their school work. So, without worrying about "experts" findings and opinions let me make my own expert observation on the value of mentoring. It is very clear to me that children who are being mentored in a positive way will improve simply because they are interacting with another mature person who cares about them and cares about what is happening to them. That's it – Just Being There has a strong, positive effect on the child's growth; educationally and personally.

We do know that children learn best when they feel safe in their learning environment.

We also know that the best learning happens when there is mutual respect.

Bonding – A Person to Person Relationship

The quality of the relationship shared by you and your Child is the most important aspect of your mentoring venture.

Essential Beliefs

You and your Child are Equals. If you see yourself as superior to your child because you are older than he is, smarter than he is, more learned than he is, or by any other measure, go find something else to do with your time. You simply are two worthy people who have come together to share a living, learning experience.

Be a Mentor for your Child. Never forget that she is a unique person. Protect her from physical and psychological abuse (including your own). Constantly let her know that you care about her regardless of the results of her performance. Learn your child's abilities to do the required skills, her readiness to do them, and her emotional and psychological status in dealing with the learning activities.

Read to your Child and have him read to you. Have him visual the stories that he hears or reads – this increases his comprehension and enjoyment. When he does a good job, don't tell him he's "Smart" – tell him he's a "Great Learner."

Become a Co-learner with your Child as she grows in her use of language. This is a great opportunity for you to learn something you don't already know. Every child that I have taught has taught me more than I have taught her. Yolanda taught me about her culture – Bobbie taught me about her music – Jordan taught me about his family's history. . .
Remember that Learning is an Active Process – both of you must be Active.
Be a Model for your Child and actively listen to him as he reads. Be there – body, mind, and soul. Share your thoughts, knowledge and feelings. If you really listen to him, you will learn more about him and about yourself.

Learn the skills involved in reading, writing, speaking, and spelling. Believe it or not, "Education Courses" are not and never have been simple courses. Learn and use whatever resources are available in seminars or in your work with other mentors. Learning is never boring. Teaching, mentoring has always been meaningful and life fulfilling for me so I will always be involved in some aspect of it – including writing.

Acknowledge and Foster the Creative Side of your Child. Creativity cannot be measured by any type of "achievement" test. Using methods that include creativity exercise the right hemisphere of the brain, are very often just plain fun, and gives her the permission and the opportunity to think. Most of all, listen to her and use her ideas.

Accept and Encourage Risking - This is for both you and your Child. You have to risk looking dumb in order to get smarter. Admit that you don't know the order of the distances of the planets from the sun and tell him that you and he will look it up. Let him take risks and don't give him negative looks and comments – he is in a safe place. Making a mistake is a signal from him to you - telling you how you can help him.

Just be human - be positive – enjoy your Child as he or she learns – enjoy yourself and enjoy being a learner.

Your Child's Education

The Real Education Process is <u>Learning</u> rather than <u>Teaching</u>

Learning is as natural as breathing. We learn from the environment around us and from the people who exist with us. We can't keep our kids from learning. So what are we as mentors to do with our kids? We take advantage of these learning opportunities and channel them into the things we call reading, writing, arithmetic, science, history, and whatever else exists.

The real value of an educational experience is the **Learning** that the child does. We can **<u>Teach</u>** until we are blue in the face, but nothing worthwhile happens until and unless the child **<u>Learns</u>**. The word "education" is derived from the Latin word "educare" which means "to bring out" or "to bring forward." What effective mentors do is to create a learning environment (physical and psychological) which enables their children to experience and internalize all types of learning experiences.

Learning by Doing

In much of your child's experiences, she has been passive in the educational process and the teacher has been the active person. In our program, the roles are different in that both the teacher and the learner are active and interactive – you and your child will be actively involved in the learning process.

One Size Does Not Fit All Children

Each of us learns in our own unique way, at our own special pace. Most learning programs are set out in a sequential, rigid pattern and the child must learn in that pattern and at the rate required to be on level or to not "get behind." Here we will require that the program be fitted to the child not the child fitted to the program. Your child will be learning the skills and information at his own pace and in his own best learning pattern.

Your child, and not the program, is at the center of the learning process.

**Let's consider the use of the term "behind' as in,
"He is behind the rest of the class."
In our class, no one is behind; everyone is exactly where he is.**

Learning Modalities

Learning involves all of the sensory modalities; Visual (seeing), Auditory (hearing), Kinesthetic (movement), Tactile (touching). Teachers often use the shortcut **VAKT** when they talk about these. This allows the mentor to use phonetic and visual learning activities backed up by the other sensory abilities. Every one of us uses all of these modalities. However, each of us uses them at different levels. Most people are Visual learners, next are the Auditory learners, then the Kinesthetic, and then the Tactile which is often used in conjunction with the Kinesthetic.

We didn't forget the fifth sense, Gustatory, the sense of taste. It doesn't come into usage in young children's learning – maybe culinary school is in your Child's future.

Opening Stage

Get acquainted with your Child – talk to her about her interests; what does she like to read, what does she watch on TV, what does she do in her spare time? Topics such as horses, bugs, baseball, rock collecting, airplanes, music, swimming, flowers, dance . . . . Go to the library with her and see what she selects – keep your preferences to yourself.

A very critical note here: You are a Co-learner with your Learner. This is an opportunity for you, the Mentor, to learn a lot about a topic you may not know much about. Working with one 4th grader on his rock collection study, I learned about the Mohs Hardness Scale and that talc is the softest rock – I didn't even know that talc is a rock.

Learning Levels and Ages of the Learner

What is your child's learning grade level? This will not be a concern. In all cases, we will be interested only in the child's personal growth and will not compare it to that of anyone else or anything else. This does include the ignoring of achievement test scores.

Let's forget about grade level or any of the other artificial levels and focus on the personal and academic growth of each of our Kids.

The Reading Program for Grades 1 - 3

THE BRITISH INFANT SCHOOL

Many of the concepts in this book are similar to those that were developed in England in their primary schools and generally called the British Infant School. While I was teaching at Elmhurst College, Dr. Ervin Schmidt, our department chairman, established a professional working relationship with the Nottingham College of Education in Nottingham, England. Several of their staff visited with us and we were able to send some of our staff to visit with them. In 1975, I had the unforgettable opportunity to make one of the visits with 14 of our students. We lived in the homes of college staff members and the students were assigned as aides in several of the elementary schools. In this way, we learned about the British Infant School program first hand.

The Infant School was created during World War II when the children were evacuated from the large cities, which were being heavily bombed, to the safer rural areas. There was neither the time nor the equipment to move the school materials; books, desks, paper, etc.; the teaching format had to be modified. Also since many of the teachers were on active duty, most of the people teaching the children had no formal training in teaching.

The learning process began with some kind of experience—perhaps taking a walk and observing the flowers. The children then drew pictures about their experience. The teacher had each child tell about her picture and then wrote what she said under the picture. These stories were the basis of each child's reading, writing, and word analysis. This led to the children writing and illustrating their own books. Art, music, poetry, and body-movement (dance) were integral parts of the total experience.

This program has been evaluated by a committee headed by Lady Plowden. Here is a commentary from the official report:

In relation to the curriculum, the Plowden Report was clear. "One of the main educational tasks of the primary school is to build on and strengthen children's intrinsic interest in learning and lead them to learn for themselves rather than from fear of disapproval or desire for praise." The report's recurring themes are individual learning, flexibility in the curriculum, the centrality of play in children's learning, the use of the environment, learning by discovery and the importance of the evaluation of children's progress - teachers should not assume that only what is measurable is valuable.

The Mentoring Model

Following is a basic model of the process that can be used in a mentoring situation. The materials are easily created or found in school supplies stores. 4 x 6 inch cards cut in two lengthwise make good Word Cards. Crayons and marking pens are also standard equipment.

An extensive description of this process for children from birth through junior high school is given in my book, *Growing and Learning,* available through the mentoring organization.

Learning Experiences – Stage 1

The first series of learning episodes begins with an actual experience by the child followed by a drawing and the child's commentary on that experience. Art is the basis for the story.

Reese and his mother, Lauren, are taking a walk in the neighborhood. Reese is observing things and Lauren is pointing things out to him. Lauren is keeping track of some of the words that seem to be interesting to Reese.

Reese: Can we get some ice cream?

Lauren: All right. Let's stop at the convenience store on the way back and get some.

Reese: (Inside the store) I like choc'lit. *

Lauren: I like chocolate, too. We'll get a pint—do you think you can carry it?

Reese: Sure, that's easy.

Lauren and Reese are now sitting at the kitchen table having their ice cream snack. Lauren gives Reese a sheet of white paper divided in half by a horizontal line and the box of crayons and says, "Draw a picture at the top here about something that happened during our walk." Reese draws a picture and, of course, it has to do with ice cream and the store.

Lauren: That's really good. Tell me about your picture. **

Reese: We went to store and I got some choc'lit ice cream. It tasted good.

Lauren writes all of those words, as exactly as possible with reasonable editing (she spells that word "c-h-o-c-o-l-a-t-e") on the bottom half of the paper. Then she says, "Let's read your story together" and she points to each word (left-to-right) and they read Reese's story (top-to-bottom). "We went to the store and bought some chocolate ice cream. It tasted good." Then she asks Reese to point to the words as they read the story again.

Lauren makes out Word Cards for these new words; store, ice cream, and bought. She adds some of the other words Reese used during the walk; sunny, cool, windy, tired, and happy. These cards will be used as Flash Cards in learning the meaning of the words and for phonics training.

Commentary

We want the interaction to be natural. Reese may want to tell the story and ramble on and on —select the heart of the story including all of the new words he is using—and then write it as close to his words as possible. Be sure to keep the new words. Pronounce and spell the words correctly, as with choc'lit. Some things have to be learned. In this case, the direction we read, left-to-right, is not natural— some cultures read from right-to-left or top-to-bottom. We will start off, right at the beginning, using the "correct" ways. Make word strips for other flavors that Reese knows. Reese will get a good look at and hear a good sound of each of these words.

*   Don't correct the pronunciation—simply use the word immediately—pronounce it correctly and spell it correctly on the file card.

**   Don't say, "What is this?" It's your child's picture—let him tell you about it.

We went to the store
and bought some
chocolate ice cream.
It tasted good.

Learning Experiences – Stage 2 – Overwriting

The second stage involves the child more in the process by her learning to write words correctly; using good penmanship. There are four forms of communication – two of them are incoming; Listening and Reading; two of them are outgoing; Speaking and Writing. Listening and Speaking are oral forms and Reading and Writing are written forms. With this story, writing by the child (penmanship) begins by the child tracing over the model presented by the mentor. Having your child read his own story is still part of the process.

We went to the park.
We saw ducks swimming.
We sat on the grass and
ate lunch.

Learning Experiences – Stage 3 – Underwriting

The third stage has the child continuing his learning correct penmanship by copying and writing below the mentor's model. He is now reading his own writing. Obviously they have just encountered Dr. Seuss's *One fish - Two fish - Red fish - Blue fish*.

The book was about

fish. Dad laughed so

hard he had to stop.

A Quick Synopsis

This has been a very quick description of a rather complex operation. The foregoing description is really all you need to know in a mentoring situation. Here is the same information in a nutshell plus some optional extensions.

The Learning Experience

This is any ordinary thing that you and your child do together. Broaden her world with experiences e.g., trips to the park, mall, library.

The Story

Write the story as it is told to you – make minor adjustments only when necessary. Use good penmanship – this is her first look at the words, make sure that she gets a correct image to store away in her brain. Read the story together, pointing to the words, going from left-to-right and top to bottom.

The Overwrite

Have her trace over the words that you wrote. Use a colored marking pen. Let her pick the color and say the name of the color. Don't worry about neatness – the small muscles are still being developed. Have her read the words as she traces them (with you and later without you).

The Underwrite

After the Overwrite, have her copy your words under your words. Use a colored marking pen. Don't criticize your child's product. Have her read the words by herself as she traces them.

The Word Strips

Print each of your child's words on a word card and file them alphabetically. Use them for Flash Cards – helps with phonics.

The Sensory Process (Excellent for a struggling child)

The child will trace the letters with her finger -- touching the paper – and say the word as many times as it takes her to trace the word – this uses the Visual, Auditory, Kinesthetic, and Tactile senses.

The Word File

File the words alphabetically. You can pull them out and clip them together in categories, e.g., one syllable words with a long vowel. You can use the word cards as "flash cards" with the words that your child knows. She will be learning phonics using her own words.

This can be used in place of the usual kinds of flash cards. Many of the words in the standard flash cards have no meaning to your child. The words in this file have an experiential meaning for her.

The Journal (Optional)

This is especially good for advanced students. You can use a blank notepad – alphabetize the pages and have your child create her own glossary of words she knows and can use correctly.

The Book (Optional)

This is the most advanced, creative activity. Your child can create and construct her own book.

The Reading Program for Grades 4 and Higher

One of my most memorable educational experiences was my visit to England in 1975 to learn more about the British Infant School. A good part of this program evolved from what I saw and learned there. Basically I saw the Learners having high quality creative learning experiences as individuals and as team members.

I have supervised hundreds of student teachers in Illinois, Texas, and Oklahoma I believe the best school I've ever seen is the Glade Hill Junior School in Nottingham, England. The students there were comparable in age to those in our middle-schools. The entire school was involved in a study of The Dance and the students were doing all kinds of art, music, poetry, and body movement activities on that topic and defining them in written and spoken language. The history of dance in the many different cultures, from the hula in Hawaii to the historical stately waltz in England, was featured in large drawings up and down the halls.

One incident remains most vivid in my mind. The Head Teacher, a Scotsman, Mr. D. A. Griffiths, very graciously invited us into his office and we were able to ask him in-depth questions about the philosophy and learning methodology in his school. He reached over and picked up a bottle of ink (fountain pens were still in use) and said, "I want my students to take a topic, for instance, this bottle, and study it thoroughly. I want them to find out all they can about glass; its origin in history, its many uses, how it is manufactured, how is it shaped, and so on. Then I want them to look at the ink; who discovered ink, what is it made of, who were the first users of ink, and so on. And then I want them to look at this metal lid and do the same. After some real study and research, they will know something about this bottle of ink."

Just think of all of the facts, skills, ideas, concepts, and understanding that would happen along with the study. It would spread out into all kinds of fields; history, mathematics, trade, chemistry, metallurgy, and on and on. And what of our learner, would she not grow in the knowledge of herself and the world around her?

Learning Units – Historical and Now

Learning Units have been with us for a long time. They were the mainstays of many of our curriculum programs in the 1950s to the 1980s – now often called The Golden Age of American Education. In my 4th and 6th grade classes we did units on Airplanes, Indians of the Southwest, The Environment, Transportation, The Planets, and European Countries. In the fourth grade, these units were usually class units – all of the children worked on the same topic although they often had different roles and learning tasks. This was a lot of individualized learning as a result of these different responsibilities. This included a lot of research, organization, creative and critical thinking, and evaluation of the findings. Late in the year, individual learning units were possible. In my sixth grade and junior high classes, the units were of the group type during most of the year followed by individual units.

A Learning Unit is essentially a research model. Children will be exploring and creating their own projects. Here we will look at the general concept of units and then explore four examples of how they have been used and how you could use them. They can be used in the regular school structure. They can be used in a summer type situation in a daily meeting with your student or in a weekly meeting. They can be used in a home-school situation. Your student can be in a group or can be learning as an individual. The process is the same and can be adapted to any situation.

The Learning Unit combines all of learning models and extends them by making the experience holistic and experiential. It also combines all the subjects in a natural way (not artificially compartmentalized as Spelling, Science, Math, etc.) so that all of the learning elements reinforce one another.

Gestalt and the Expanding Horizons

Gestalt is a really great German word meaning wholeness, completeness, the entire set of factors coming together. You know that "The whole is greater than the sum of the parts." We use that concept and other ideas such as "All learning is interrelated".

Don't be concerned when your child seems to dwell on one topic or concept. Knowledge expands from one concept to many others. It's the nature of Intellectual Inquiry that when we study and read and think, we naturally move into wider and wider circles of knowledge and interest. It is also true that the Mentor can give his child more and more experiences that will add to the knowledge and interests of that child.

Every topic has an almost unlimited number of options of inquiry spanning; areas in history mathematics, literature, music, science, et al. We will explore some of these options in the different examples below. The results can be visualized as a concentric set of circles with the child's name in the center circle.

YOUR CHILD'S EXPANDING WORLD

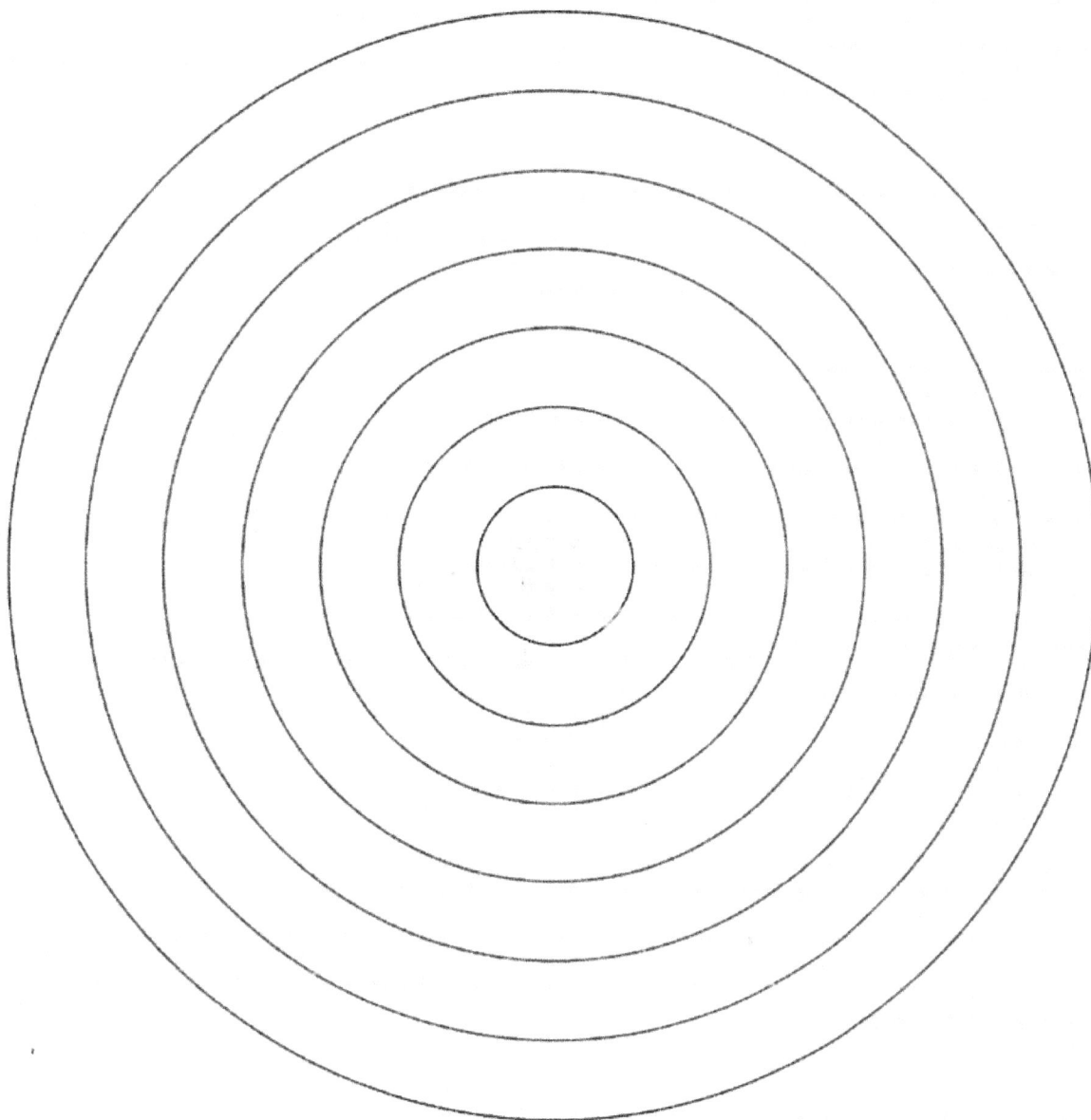

Your child's name will be placed in the center circle.

The Jordan Project

Jordan was ten years old and going into the fourth grade. In the summer of 2015, he was attending an eight week summer Project: Transformation program that included a variety of recreational and educational activities. The program was located at a local church and volunteers from that church assisted the children in all areas and especially in the reading aspect. The children had a 45 minute reading session daily. Most of the volunteers had not been teachers. The people assisting with the activities were college students who were serving internships giving them hands-on service experiences with children.

Early in the reading sessions, the church volunteer working with Jordan became concerned with his lack of interest in reading and with his odd behavior which featured the use of different types of voice impressions as he read. Earlier in the year, I had spoken with directors of the educational program at the church; my wife Bobbie was the choir director; and had given them a copy of my book, *Growing and Learning*. They thought that I might be able to help Jordan so they asked me to spend some time with him.

I met with Miss Kat, the intern who was supervising the reading program. Miss Kat is a junior level student majoring in Education at Oklahoma City University. She was extremely helpful in our work with Jordan. She was able to supervise the program with very little help from me.

In our first meeting, in response to my question, Jordan expressed his interest in playing basketball and in following professional basketball teams; especially the OKC Thunder and the recent title tournament. Miss Kat found four books on basketball in the program library and information on the local Thunder team. I started our sessions having conversations with Jordan using pictures of the title games cut out of my *Sports Illustrated* issues. I had Jordan tell me about one of the pictures and I wrote out what he said and asked him to read it. This was the first of several spoken/written discussions and the beginning of a journal. (When a child draws a picture or is presented by a picture, the correct inquiry is "Tell me about your picture." or "Tell me about this picture.").

One of our library books was a history of the beginning of the game of basketball with its creation by James Naismith. Jordan was very interested in this avenue of study and we completed the entire book. As we talked, we got into the equipment (the first basket was a peach basket), the reason the game was invented, the playing area, the ball, the first rules, etc. Jordan got interested in the rules and the playing space – so we spent most of the rest of our sessions on these topics with journal entries to match.

Jordan read all four of books and we discussed different aspects of basketball.

Our final creation was a scale drawing of a modern professional type basketball court with notations on the 10 second rule, the three point line, free throw line, etc. We made several copies of this drawing and Jordan proudly took one home and gave others to staff members.

Throughout the sessions, more than 50 hand-printed flash cards of new vocabulary words and old words needing reinforcement were created and used. Some phonics learning took place with recognition of some letter patterns.

Jordan's interest in the project grew very quickly and stayed high during the entire time. He came eagerly to every session. Since I had other responsibilities, Miss Kat supervised many of these sessions. She maintained the energy and I always came back to an improved and happier Jordan. At the final award session, Jordan was acknowledged for his growth and performance.

Results:

Jordan: His knowledge was generally expanded and deepened.

His interest in the topic was broadened.

Learning became stronger part of the learner's life.

The learner had great experiences with two caring adult mentors.

The learner learned new words and known words were reinforced.

Mentors: He learned more about the topic.

He had a great interpersonal experience.

She also had a great interpersonal experience and gained a new learning model.

Susan's Expanding World

Now I will go back into my own history with learning units. I learned about them as a fourth grade teacher in the Barrington, Illinois, school district in 1955. The Barrington school system was quite famous – many teachers and administrators from the United States and foreign countries visited us to see what we were doing. We teachers were encouraged to have our children learn using whole class learning units. Children in my class studied the Southwestern States and Airplanes as class units. I decided that for our final unit each of my children would choose his or her own topic. Rocks, trucks, burros, were among the chosen topics.

Susan was one of the 29 children in my class. She was really interested in horses. As she read all of the books in our school library about horses; she learned about their role in the history of the West, the different breeds and uses, their interaction with people, etc. Susan has always wanted to own a horse. Among other books, she read *My Friend Flicka* by Mary O'Hara. *Black Beauty*, by Anna Sewell was a bit of a stretch for her – the words are not all easy to read and the concepts are sometimes hard to understand. However, Susan did well – a book that a child is reading to learn is usually a "stretcher" – there are new words and ideas to move up on.

When she selected her topic for her individual study unit, Susan decided to compose a book based on horses (no surprise) and I did not try to change her to "something new". Her inquiring mind began with an interest in "The Horse" as a concept and spread naturally and inevitably into many other areas. She subsequently chose and created a terrific report on *The Evolution of the Horse*.

It is also true that the Teacher becomes more expert in the process. We learned a lot more about horses as we traveled with Susie on her quest for finding all about the evolution of the horse. Did you know that the *eohippus* had four toes on its front feet and three toes on its hind feet? I didn't either – to tell the truth I learned a lot more than that while working with her and reading her report.

An example of a previous Individualized Reading Session with Susan

Every stage in this process is an exploring stage. We are simply using this step to have Susan explore the different aspects of the horse concept. We need to have her look at a lot of different "horse" areas. Just be careful to start where she is.

"Tell me about Flicka, Susan." (This is the start of the writing phase. She is creating a journal   with her new words and thoughts.)

"Flicka is a horse that Katy found. He is a mustang. Katy wants to keep him but her dad doesn't want him around his tame horses."

"What is a 'mustang'?"

"I'm not sure. I think it's some kind of wild horse."

"Let's look it up in the encyclopedia." (*Now we have are computers and Wikipedia but having the pages all open and right there makes this research easier.*)

"Check to see if it's in this list of horse terms, Susan."

"Here it is – 'Mustang is a wild horse of the Western plains, descended from Spanish horses.'

I know what 'wild' and 'plains' mean – I don't know what 'descended' or 'Spanish' mean"

"While we're here, let's copy the horse terms you already know from this list."

"I know wild, plains, colt, filly, mare, and pony."

"O. K., that's enough encyclopedia for now. Read some of your Flicka book to me now."

Before we finish this session, we have Susan make entries into her journal. The words would include *Flicka, mustang,* and *corral,* from her story and *descended, plains, Spanish, colt, filly, mare, and pony* from the encyclopedia. We are including some words she already knows with new words she learned in context today – these are "her words" – they belong to her.

Francisco

Recently I became a mentor to Francisco. Francisco is the son of parents from Guatemala. His parents spoke Spanish at home but English was his first language. In our first session, he told me that he liked soccer and that he played the flute. I told him that he and I were going to write a book together and I asked him which of these topics he wanted to write about first. He chose soccer.

The first book he selected from our library featured stories on 20 of the most famous players in the world – from 12 different countries. I brought in a National Geographic world map and a world globe. As he read each of the stories, we located the country on the map and I marked it with a label with the player's name on it. We also located the country on the globe and checked the direction and distance from our location in Oklahoma.

I also contacted my friend, Peter McGahey. Peter is head coach of the woman's soccer team at Central Michigan University. He and I set up a pen pal connection for Francisco with one of his players. She was from Canada. They began a correspondence that lasted quite a while. The letters were funneled through Peter and me. Francisco and I made a label for Michigan on our map and located it in relationship to our location.

Francisco kept a log of his activities in a journal. Unfortunately, through a personal concern, the mentoring experience ended after six months and I never got to work with him on the flute aspect of the project.* He and I (and his parents) agreed that we had had a great experience working together.

Other Topics for Individual Learning Units

Working with your student you and he can choose any topic for his research and use any process that fits the situation. Some units are; Poets and Poetry, The Trail of Tears, The Olympics, The History of Measurement, Our Town, the Aquarium-an eco-system, Any Sports, Animals (pets and otherwise), The Arts (Music, Art, Dance from various countries), the Planets, Antarctica, and on and on.

Some of the best units relate to what is happening at the present time. For example, if it is the year of the Summer or Winter Olympics, there are terrific opportunities for Geography and Map Study - Where participants come from - Flags of each nation and symbols in the flags). Math - Measurement - Distances – Lengths. Spelling and Vocabulary - New words and Roots, e.g., slalom, biathlon, luge. Reading (History of the Olympics - The Summer Olympics).

* In December of 2015, my wife, Bobbie Bullard Pierro, was diagnosed with brain cancer. She courageously battled with this condition for the following year and a half.

The Learner

"We can only help an equal."
—Gerald Jampolsky

The Most Important Players in the Game

What we believe about our children determines what we will do with them in our society and more specifically, in our schools. If we make them the most important players in the game, we will base our efforts and our dreams for the future on them. We will place their Needs, their Aspirations, and their Futures first on our priority list.

If we place our Power, our Money, our Egos somewhere else, our children become pawns in the game. They become objects – in business language, they are "widgets," objects to buy, to sell, to discard, or to use in whatever way that fulfills the goals of the users. So, right here and now, we have to declare our values, our beliefs, our focusing, our own futures on what our children are and what we declare to be best for them in all areas of their lives, and specifically, in our schools. Here are my beliefs about children – the bases for what I have done as a teacher.

Children are Living Learners

When we say, or in some other way, communicate to them that they are not sufficient, we are missing the reality of what growing and living must be. Children are living learners. They are accomplishing what they can and will do. We can't judge them by what we would want them to be or what we expect them to do.

Here are my beliefs about our Learners. I also believe that they succeed best when their growth includes a relationship with caring, committed Mentors; parents and teachers.

Basic Beliefs about People (Children are People)

I am unique; there is not now, never has been, and never will be another person exactly like me.
I am a seeker of knowledge; self-knowledge and knowledge about the outside world.
I am a total person; mental, physical, psychological, social, emotional, aesthetic, and spiritual.
I am a worthwhile person.
I am a loving, caring person.
I have a miraculous, creative mind.
I have vast, untapped potential.
I have God given, human rights to live, to laugh, to love, and to be free.

I set my own personal goals for success and I expect to achieve them.

I possess great personal qualities; desire, dedication, determination, confidence, pride, and courage.

I take risks in order to grow and to learn.

I am a dreamer.

I am totally responsible for who I am, for what I do, and for how I feel.

I have the responsibility to assist others in reaching their goals.

I am persistent in my striving to reach my goals; I never, never give up.

I expect and welcome the changes that come into my life.

I believe in a Supreme Wisdom which sustains me and enriches my life.

The Qualities of the Learner

In this section, I have chosen four of the qualities that children possess that are especially critical in a learning setting. Of course, these qualities are critical for us adults as well. It is absolutely essential that the people in charge of our children's education believe that children possess these qualities. This means that children are people, and, as Jampolsky implies, we can't assist them in their growth if we believe that they are less than we are.

Quality #1 - Uniqueness

"Why should we be in such desperate haste to succeed, and in such desperate enterprises?

If a man does not keep pace with his companions, perhaps it is because he hears a different drummer.

Let him step to the music which he hears, however measured or far away."
—Henry David Thoreau

There are many basic beliefs that are self-evident and the most self-evident is that each of us is a unique individual. There are no two individuals who are exactly alike. There is not now, never has been, and never will be a person exactly like you. Nature has gone to great lengths to create the infinite number of different snowflakes, roses, blades of grass, coyotes, etc. Nature must cherish this quality to have taken such pains to create a new mold for every entity. She didn't leave you out of her creations.

This uniqueness is not limited to the physical aspects. Each of us has a unique set of behavior traits and patterns. We have had different experiences and have developed different perceptual views. We are all different and each of us sees the world differently. We see success in a very personal, unique way. My measures of success may be a real turnoff for you, as yours may be for me.

The world of education is a vital part of the experiences of a child. He enters school as a unique individual; he learns each new fact or concept in his own unique way, through his own unique perceptual screens; he continually creates this unique self. The process of education creates the logical impossibility of each child becoming more unique. Is it not possible that the purpose of education is the continuous creation of a unique individual? I believe that it is.

"Since the process of education results in the creation of increased uniqueness, isn't it obvious that the purpose of education is this creation of uniqueness."

Quality #2 - The Seeker

"Ask, and it shall be given you; seek and ye shall find;
knock, and it shall be opened unto you.
For everyone that asketh, receiveth; and he that seeketh, findeth;
and to him that knocketh it shall be opened."
—Matthew 7:7, 8

The process of learning is seeking. We are seekers of knowledge, not sponges soaking up facts. Have you observed a kitten, a puppy, a baby exploring the world? That is the process of learning; the model from which we can learn. Children drive us crazy with their questions – isn't that terrific?! They want to learn. Where does the turn-off come from? So many of our children have been ignored, insulted, even punished for their inquiring minds. Education, the formal type, has progressively degenerated into "Sit still, be quiet, answer the questions, fill in the spaces." I recall clearly how Doris Nash, the headmistress of the Sea Mills Infant School at Bristol, England, stated this, "The two most natural things children do is to talk and to move. And the first things they hear in our schools is 'sit still and be quiet'."

The very best learning that I have observed in schools has been done in a busy, relaxed, stimulating, and, yes, a disciplined environment. Respect was present. Self-discipline was the major goal in the 'behavior' game.

Quality #3 - The Total Person

"Hey, you've got a flat tire."

"No problem, it's only flat on the bottom."
—An Anonymous Sage

We are complete, whole, total people. We are:

Physical - We have a physical body which we nourish through exercise, diet, activity, and rest.

Mental - We have a mind which we use to learn more about ourselves and the social and physical world in which we exist.

Social - We are social beings who relate to others in a multitude of ways.

Aesthetic - We are aware of many types of beauty in our world; music, art, literature, and body movement.

Emotional - We have emotions that express themselves across a wide spectrum, from despair to total joy.

Spiritual - We are spiritual people who have strong beliefs about a Supreme Being, whatever that concept may mean to us.

Psychological - Each of us is aware of our own 'self.'

Family Members - Each of us has a feeling of membership to our roots.

Creative - We use our mental abilities to create new forms; new, even if they are new only to ourselves.

Sometimes in our desire to teach those kids everything they are supposed to know, we forget that they are complex, complicated people. It is simplistic to think that all we have to do is "sit 'em down and larn 'em". That mental aspect of a child can be influenced so much by all those other aspects.

Joey is taking a test knowing that his dog is being treated at the veterinarian's clinic and Beth is writing a poem while listening to a Rachmaninoff concerto. Are their performances being affected by other forces? We are not dealing with disembodied, unemotional heads. There have been times in the history of schools that this was the pre-eminent belief. From the 1950s through the 1980s, we spoke about "The Whole Child" and I believe we were in the right arena.

Quality #4 - The Risk Taker

"A ship in the harbor is safe,

but that is not what ships are built for."
—Poster in the Church Hall

Of all the messages that appear on posters, in wisdom sayings in old adages, in the human potential books, the most frequent and most ardent is the one on taking risks and learning through our mistakes. The adult world believes it. Business leaders swear by it. Sales people are taught to learn and grow with it. Here is a story told by Rita Davenport:

"When I was learning to ski, I told my instructor, "I'm doing well. I didn't fall once." My instructor replied, "Then you didn't try hard enough." (Her goal was not to fall, rather than learning how to ski better.)

From a speech given by my friend, Barbara Davies, I learned that:

"Anything worth doing is worth doing poorly - at first. We don't do things perfectly right off the bat. We make mistakes as we learn and the more important and difficult the skill, the more 'mistakes' we must expect and allow for."

Creativity is the ultimate form of risking. You are out there all by yourself in the unknown. And, it's a lot easier and less scary if you know that someone who cares about you is there to support you, to commiserate with you in your setbacks, and to celebrate with you in your triumphs.

The Mentor/Learner

Remember that you as a mentor (and a person) also have all of the qualities given above.

Only when we have love, appreciation, understanding, and dedicated caring for whom we are, can we have the same for others. When we see ourselves in this light, it allows us to see others in the same light. Then we are equals and only then will we give what we actually have inside our being.
—Bobbie B. Pierro, Gifted Musician

Growth, Development, and Readiness

Maturation

The child is constantly confronted with the nagging question: "What are you going to be?" Courageous would be the youngster who could look the adult squarely in the face and say, "I'm not going to be anything; I already am.@ We adults would be shocked by such an insolent remark, for we have forgotten, if indeed we ever knew, that a child is an active, participating and contributing member of society from birth. Childhood isn't a time when he is molded into a human who will then live life; he is a human who is living life. No child will miss the zest and joy of living unless these are denied him by adults who convinced themselves that childhood is a period of preparation.

—David Elkind, *The Hurried Child*

We must be concerned about the possible dangers of "pushing down" the elementary school curriculum into the very early years of a child's life. Third graders are now asked to do what was formerly done in the fourth grade – Second graders are now asked to do what was formerly done in the third grade; etc. By doing so, schools and parents alike are using developmentally inappropriate instructional and learning practices that will distort the smooth development of learning of their children.

Children need to have many and varied experiences to develop in a healthy way. Schools and parents pushing their infants and children to learn at earlier and earlier ages does not allow a child time to have the "rich" experiences necessary to absorb and learn in a deep and meaningful way.

It is essential that children learn what they are intellectually and experientially ready to learn. Teachers and curriculum experts have decided that the kids should learn the concept of double negatives in the fifth grade. This is how I learned about it. I was teaching a fourth grade class about this concept and did everything I and the text materials had to have them learn, "If you don't have nothing, you must have something." Nothing worked – the heads kept shaking. Well, I finally gave up and figured it would come up again later. Well, it did. A few years later, I was teaching a sixth grade class. The concept in this textbook was double negatives. I said to the kids, "If you don=t have nothing, you must have something." They looked at me with this, "So, what else is new?" look - with the tilt of the head and all. So, this concept is too hard for ten year olds and too easy for twelve year olds. Then we should introduce it to them when they are 11 years old.

Readiness

**Every child is ready to learn something—it's our job as teachers
and parents to determine what that child is ready to learn.**
—James Hymes

Many parents try to teach their children skills and strategies that they are not ready or able to learn. One of my favorite psychologists, James Hymes, made this situation very simple. His quote above tells the whole story. Our program requires that our parents keep in close touch with their children throughout their growing and learning so they know when the time is right.

In college, I learned about E. L. Thorndike's three Laws of Readiness and I translated them to fit my teaching and coaching models. I also added a fourth law that I think is really crucial. Here are those laws as they pertain to somebody's daughter "Sarah" and her progress in learning:

1. **If Sarah is ready to learn to read and she is allowed to read, she will have a happy experience.**

2. **If Sarah is ready to learn to read and she is not allowed to read, she will be frustrated.**

3. **If Sarah isn't ready to learn how to read and she is forced to read, she will have a negative, perhaps even a traumatic experience.**

Number 1 is the ideal situation. Sarah is ready to learn read—you are ready to have her read—and everyone is happy. Number 2 happens quite often. Sarah is ready to read—she wants to read—but someone or something is not allowing her or helping her and she is feeling unhappy about it. (Have you ever sat on the bench, itching to get into the ball game, and the coach ignored you—he said you weren't ready but you knew you were ready?)

Number 3 is the really scary one. This is the one that brings out verbal abuse and the insults. Sarah is just not able to learn the skills of reading and her parents are not willing for that to be O. K. They keep pushing her, abusing her. "You're not even trying." "Our neighbor's daughter is younger than you and she's reading."

They are not willing to wait a little while until Sarah has developed physically to the place that she can do the task. Sarah has known those traumatic episodes in which Mom and Dad pushed and shoved her to do things and being abusive to her, making her feel guilty or an embarrassment to her family when she wasn't able to do them.

Here is my idea for a fourth law:

4. **If Sarah isn't ready to learn how to read, she is not forced to read and that's O.K. and she's O.K.**

Here we have reasonable, intelligent, caring parents who accept Sarah right where she is and deal with her in terms of what she can do and what she can't do.

These are the parents who wait patiently for her to take her first steps, to be able to use the bathroom by herself, etc. This is the coach who told you to let your child grow a little more before you stuck that bat into his hands.

Defeat Experiences

A child who is required to do work at levels above her maturation status and readiness level will experience defeat and failure. Common attitudes developed by such a child are: "I've never been good in math" – "I'm just not smart enough to be a good reader."

Tony learned in kindergarten that he couldn't do the required work so he had to stay there another year. His fourth grade achievement test scores which made him repeat that grade proved to him that he wasn't a sufficient learner. As many others, he quit psychologically in the sixth grade and dropped out of high school when he became legally old enough. What a waste!

Our children in this program will learn at the level that they can learn – they will be compared only to their own ability levels and not to others children or to pre-conceived levels set for all children.

Process and Product

How a child learns *what* she is expected to learn is crucial to that learner's growth and development. *How* refers to the Process of Learning – *What* refers to the Product of Learning. In this section we will look at the way these concepts are used and the possibilities for their usage.

Let's examine the roles of Process and Product in a common school situation. Learning about magnets is one of the topics in the 5th grade science curriculum in the Alpha City School System.

The Product Model and Magnets Teaching Experience

Georgia Flanders at the Monroe School has her kids read the five pages in the text book on magnets and she gives them a pretty good lecture on north and south poles and the rest of the information on those pages. She gives them worksheets to take home for "homework" with questions about what they learned from the reading – worksheets are a required part of the course of study in all concepts being taught. She will include her lecture and their reading on the weekly test.

That really is all there is to it. The children have learned about magnets. It was quick and efficient. It was impersonal and it was shallow.

The Process Model and Magnets Learning Experience

Martha McClure at the Main Street School does it this way:

She divides her class into working pairs. She has prepared worksheets entitled Bar Magnets, Round Magnets, and Horse Shoe Magnets. "Okay, here are your directions. I won't repeat them, so pay attention. I'm giving a magnet to one member of your set. I'm giving the other member a worksheet for that kind of magnet. As a team, you will try out your magnet on different materials in this room to see if it is attracted to them. That includes other magnets. One person handles the magnet, the other takes notes. After ten minutes, you will trade magnets with someone, get a worksheet for that kind of magnet, and change handling and note taking. Ten minutes later, swap magnets so you will have the third kind of magnet. Decide who will take notes, first. Flip a coin if you can't agree. Any questions?"

Everybody gets busy until:

"Stop, we're through. Take your seats. All right, let's take bar magnets first. What did you find out?" The findings are reported and noted on the board so the students can get that information into their science journals. They will be tested on what they learn on their weekly test. They have the facts available to answer any and all questions.

Teaching and Learning

Miss Flanders is doing the standard, lecture-read method – she is teaching the kids about magnets. The students are passive – reacting to her teaching. They are reading about a scientific concept. It's quick, it's efficient - it's shallow, it's boring. They'll be able to pass the weekly test and they're ready to answer the questions about magnets that may be included in the standardized achievement test. They won't be asked how they learned that the north pole of one bar magnet attracts the south pole of another bar magnet.

Mrs. McClure is using the Discovery Method. The children are active - they are experiencing the learning. It's slow, it's effective, it's meaningful. The children have used and learned a process that they will be able to use in their future study of science and other fields. They will also be able to pass the weekly test and they're ready to answer the questions about magnets that may be included in the standardized achievement test. They won't be asked how they learned that the north pole of one bar magnet attracts the south pole of another bar magnet even though they did find this out while they were experimenting.

If you give a man a fish, he eats for a day;
If you teach a man to fish, he eats for the rest of his life.

So:

If you are taught a fact, you might be able to remember it
and pass the next test.
If you learn how it works, you can use it as you want to
and even be creative with it.

It's the difference between Learning and Teaching. Miss Flanders was *Teaching* them – Mrs. McClure was having them *Learn*. Miss Flanders was *Indoctrinating* them – Mrs. McClure was *Educating* them. Joanne, in Mrs. McClure's room, has that whole experience of having the north pole of the magnet being attracted by the south pole and rejected by the north pole in her memory banks along with all the thoughts and feelings that accompanied the learning activity.

Was I in _Jeopardy_? The TV show, that is?

Recently, I was playing golf by myself and I ran into Jerry. He was also playing by himself so we decided to join up. After the usual pleasantries including my confessing to be a former teacher and college professor, Jerry said, "I don't know what we're teaching our kids these days. We were having a conversation the other day and my nephew didn't know anything about Hannibal crossing the Alps with elephants and defeating the Romans."

I am now smart enough and comfortable enough in my old age to not try convincing Jerry that there is no way for our schools to teach everyone every fact in history, science, math, and the arts. I could have asked him how important Hannibal was relative to knowing more about the history of the World. Was it as important as knowing about the Trail of Tears, or about the placing of Japanese-Americans in detention camps during WWII, or life during The Great Depression – or going to Europe and knowing about the defeat of the Spanish Armada and the signing of the Magna Carta – or for expanding and learning about Marco Polo's travels and the Inca, Mayan, and Aztec civilizations.

This falls in the category of Product, that is, <u>what</u> we learn and we want to focus on Process; <u>how</u> we learn.

Comprehension and Context

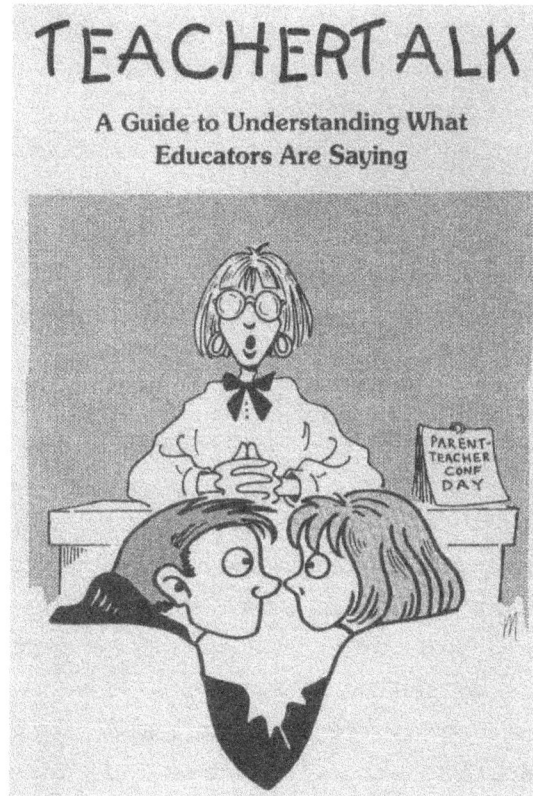

TEACHERTALK

A Guide to Understanding What Educators Are Saying

PARENT-TEACHER CONF DAY

Teacher: After evaluating Timmy's *percentile-ranked scores* on the norm-referenced readiness test and his grade equivalent scores on the local criterion-referenced battery, the Principal and I have determined that the best placement for him is in our homogeneous, ability-grouped, transitional first grade.

Parents: Huh?

Comprehension

Do you think those parents were receiving what the teacher was sending? They may have understood each and every word but they probably didn't have the slightest idea what to do or why they should do it. It held no meaning for them.

We want Renee to understand what she reads. If the words she is "reading" are not part of her working vocabulary—if the sentences she is "reading" have no meaning to her, then she is not reading; she is making sounds. So, when she writes a word or meets a new word, we want it to be in a context that will enable her to understand what she has read.

In order to be an independent reader, Renee has to be in control of the skills that make reading clear and understandable. We want her to be able to read without us being there so she needs to be able to get meaning (comprehension) from the text and by using the dictionary and the encyclopedia.

Comprehension—that's what reading and writing are all about. When I write a letter to you, it is my hope that what I write and what you read have the same meaning. When your child reads a book, you hope that he understands the story exactly the same way the author intended it to be understood.

If we don't know what the person was communicating in his writing, we have not read the material—even if we know what all the words mean.

There is another strong tool that Renee has at her disposal—it's called Context and it makes use of Context Clues. You have been conducting a unit on animals and their young and your children have learned that a young cow is a calf, a young horse is a colt, a young dog is a puppy, a young cat is a kitten, and so on. You want to expand their vocabulary with some new terms and concepts, so you write the word **cygnet** on the board and begin the lesson:

"Do you know what a cygnet is?" No hands are raised. "I'm going to write a story on the board that has the word, cygnet, in it. Raise your hand when you know what a cygnet is."

"Kristan loved to look out over the pond at her grandmother's farm."

"Any ideas? (Some given by children – one having to do with something in the pond is accepted.)

"This was especially great early in the morning."

"Any more thoughts? No, let's go on.

"This morning she saw a line of little cygnets swimming."

"Yes, you are getting close - it is an animal that lives in a pond. We are not done, yet."

"Behind their mother."

"All right, it's a baby animal. But what kind of animal is it?" (More guesses.)

"A great white swan."

"Good, you have worked it out – A cygnet is a baby swan. Now you have a new word to put into your journal."

The children learned a new word with its meaning and were involved in the learning process – they used Context Clues. Here, if the children are ready for it, you could do a phonetic lesson on the word cygnet.

The y is a vowel, taking the place of an i.

The y is in a closed syllable so the i is short.

The g is followed by a consonant so it has the hard sound.

The e in an unaccented, closed syllable so it has a schwa sound.

Reading to and Asking Questions

We really encourage you to read to your child during each session. Read stories and poems and talk about what they are telling you—what they mean to you. Ask good questions. He will ask questions. Encourage this questioning and answer each question thoroughly and relative his understanding. Have him close his eyes as you read to him and have him "see" the story. And have him visualize stories as he reads them.

Creativity and Critical Thinking

It is nothing short of a miracle that the modern methods of instruction have not entirely strangled the holy curiosity of inquiry; for this delicate little plant, aside from stimulation stands mainly in the need of freedom; without this it goes to wrack and ruin without fail.

— Albert Einstein

Kinds of Thinking

There are two types of thinking involved in dealing with a problem or situation:
1. Convergent Thinking - Objective
2. Divergent Thinking – Creative and Critical

Convergent Thinking asks this question: "What is the correct answer?"

Available information → → → Correct Answer

Divergent Thinking asks this question: "What are the possibilities?"

Available information → → → Possible Answers

For a lot of our work with kids, we want them to think about the possible answers and then to select the best choice. That=s not the best approach when doing multiple-choice items. We want them to go directly to finding the best answer, filling in that circle, and moving on.

Creativity Can't be Measured

Let me begin this item by saying, "If your child is taking a standardized achievement test, tell him to leave his creative mind at the classroom door. Tell him to answer the question and don't keep thinking about the possibilities." Creative type thinking can get you into trouble while you are taking a multiple-choice type test. You are more apt to choose an answer that doesn't agree with the writer's best answer. Also, you will slow down your responses, lose time, and not complete the test.

It is extremely important that you keep broadening the world and the mind of your child. Many studies have shown:

Students who study music do significantly better work in math than other students. In fact, all areas of the Arts; music, art, literature, poetry; improve the effectiveness of the thinking process.

Creative thinking (a modern term is "Thinking outside of the Box.") is essential for optimum use of the brain.

There are different types of brain activity in the left and the right hemispheres of the brain. Generally, left brain activity is organized and linear - right brain activity is creative and inquiring.

It is essential that both hemispheres of the brain be developed - they're designed to be complementary.

Creativity-Inquiry and Fact-Recall

Fact-Recall-Informational Learning asks, "What's the right answer?" This is limited thinking - the type used in achievement testing.

Creativity-Inquiry asks, "What are the possibilities?" No limits and testable only in an interaction with someone who is knowledgeable about the topic - especially a mentor.

Standardized Testing is mainly based on Fact-Recall thinking.

Example of using Divergent Thinking and Convergent Thinking

As usual, these kinds of learning happen naturally and need not be forced. Just be aware that they exist and can be recognized and utilized. And - they won't happen if you close down your life space and your child=s life space B **Explore, Explore, Explore!**

A Creative Way to Solve a Math Problem - Is this O.K.?

Lauren is discussing her grade on the weekly test with her math teacher, Mr. Strict.

The Problem:

The Super Sales hardware store was having a ASuper Sale@. Their humidifier listed at $52 was being sold for $25. How much lower was the sales price than the usual price? Show your work.

Lauren: AI got the right answer. Why did you give me three points instead of five points?

Mr. Strict: The correct way to do this problem is:

$$\begin{array}{r} 52 \\ -25 \\ \hline 27 \end{array}$$

And this is the work you showed: 5 - 2 = 3, 3 x 9 = 27. That is the right answer, but you didn't get it the right way. In fact, I don't know how you got it. I think you were guessing.

Lauren: My Grampa taught me that two figure numbers reverse themselves in multiples of nine and the multiplier is the difference between the numbers. There's a difference of 3 between 2 and 5, so the correct answer is 3 x 9 = 27. That's a different way to do it and it's a correct way.

There were 20 word problems on the test. Each was worth 5 points using the Perfection Grading scale. She read the question correctly but she didn't solve it the 'right' way. She got the right answer and was able to give the problem a legitimate mathematical treatment.

Actually, if this were my classroom, I would give her 2 bonus points for going off on her own to improve her learning and for helping me expand my mind.

Critical Thinking

A multiple-choice test usually has dozens of questions or "items." For each item, the test-taker is supposed to *select* the "best" choice among a set of four or five options. They are sometime called "selected-response tests."

Let's start with this item:

Which one of these game balls does not belong with the others?
    A. Basketball
    B. Soccer Ball
    C. Football   *
    D. Baseball
* The "best" answer. The other answer options are called "distractors."

This is where the fun begins - the obvious answer is the football and the shape of the ball, prolate versus regular sphere has been the factor in that decision. But you have Jose and Tracey in your classroom.

Jose is shortstop on his Little League team so he thinks about it. He lets his creative juices flow and he says to himself, "The baseball - It's the only ball that isn't filled with air."

Tracey, an equally critical thinker and soccer star, says to herself, "I really want the soccer ball to be the answer, so, let's see . . . all of the other balls have only one color - my soccer ball has black and white sections."

Meanwhile, back at Testing Center, they will be noting, "The statistics show that more than half of the children who answer this item say that the answer is football, so that's the *best* answer."

So, both Tracey and Jose are "wrong."

It really would have been fair to these two critical thinkers had the stem read this way:

Which one of these game balls has a shape different from the others?

Multiple-choice items are best used for checking whether students have learned facts and routine procedures that have one, clearly correct answer. They work best in math where you don=t get to have an opinion about the best answer for the square root of 64. However, an item may have two reasonable answer options. Therefore, test directions usually ask test takers to select the "best" answer. If, on a reading test, a student selected a somewhat plausible answer, does it mean that she cannot read, or that she does not see things exactly the way the test maker does?

In items in History, it's safe to ask which amendment to the constitution changes the voting age requirement from 21 to 18 years (it's the 26th amendment). However, you will not find a test item that asks you what age you think should be required for voting and then gives you four choices.

Test-makers often promote multiple-choice tests as "objective." This is because there is no human judgment in the scoring, which usually is done by machine. However, humans decide what questions to ask, how to phrase questions, and what "distractors" to use. All these are subjective decisions that can be biased in ways that unfairly reward or harm some test-takers. Therefore, multiple-choice tests are not really objective - they ask for Convergent Thinking.

What Should We Do?

Let me repeat it: Leave your imagination at the door when you enter the room to take an 'objective test.' You have to think the way the test makers think, so choose the answer that jumps out at you, fill in the circle, and move on. If you follow the kind of thinking that Tracey and Jose did, you will also be using up a lot of time - time you can't afford to waste.

Descriptive and Normative Assessments

Fortunately, we mentors do not have the odious, difficult, even impossible job of grading kids A, B, C, D, and F; or 77, 83, 91, and 100; or 89th percentile, 62nd percentile, and 99th percentile.

Normative Assessment

Normative assessment is the assigning of a number or a letter to a student's action or activity. This is usually done in grading papers, giving test scores, and marking check lists. A report card with only letter grades is an example of normative usage. In our dealings with Standardized Achievement Testing we use only normative terms; e.g., Eddie's score on the reading test was at the 67th percentile.

Descriptive Assessment

The great majority of a teacher's and all of mentor's assessments are descriptive. This is done only with descriptive words, e.g., "You have really worked hard on this project and the result is terrific!" "This paper is not as neat as it should be." At a parent/teacher session, "Paula's work has greatly improved during this quarter. Her book report was especially well done."

Happily, we mentors never have to compare the work of our student with that of the other children in the group. To Francisco, Susan, Jordan, and others, I could say, "That's great! Your work is getting better all the time."

"Objective" Grading

People like to think that giving grades is objective. We think that when one teacher grades a paper, he is giving it the same treatment and evaluation (that is, grade) as every other teacher. This is not even close to being true.

Years ago, a study was done to determine how true this belief is. Copies of a high school student's English theme were sent out to thousands of high school English teachers to be graded. The result was that this same theme was graded from A through F. There were variations based on grammar, spelling, using the more exact words, creativity, feelings expressed, etc.

So the same researchers said, "Let's try a math test. That should be more objective." It wasn't – the grades varied from A to F. Not all teachers scored the answers to be either completely right or completely wrong. On an item worth 5 points, some teachers always gave wrong answers 0 points. Some teachers gave some credit for setting up the solution correctly or doing the correct computations; they "took off some points."

Book Reports

THE CREATION AND EVOLUTION OF
66 WAYS TO REPORT ON A BOOK

There will be times when you may want your student to give you some feedback on the book he has read. A one-on-one discussion is the usual process but why not mix it up a little with an interesting option. Let me suggest a possibility. Way back in Ancient History (Actually 1956-57), I was teaching a 4th grade class in Barrington, Illinois. The Barrington School District was one of the finest in the country. People came from all over the world to see what we were doing with Individualized Reading, Learning Centers, Units of Learning, and much more. We were creative, child-centered, arts-oriented, and just plain committed to children's learning and growth.

One day, I announced to my class that we would be doing book reports and the cries of dismay echoed off the walls. So I said to myself, "This is the time for a brainstorming session." So I called for a special class meeting. (We had regular class meetings on Monday mornings and Friday afternoons). The students were very clear that the standard book report (The Title, Author, Main Characters approach) was boring, a waste of time, and far less than a learning experience. So I said, "What do we do?" and we came up with the idea, "What are some other ways to report on a book?" we came up with 21 ways to report on a book. Susie built a diorama to illustrate her book that featured a queen, Kevin made a display of model trucks with materials from his dad's auto dealership after reading about trucks, and Roger brought in his baseball glove and bat and showed us how Lou Gehrig would have played according to his book.

While I was Curriculum Director at Glen Ellyn, Illinois, Junior High School, Marge Crawford, an outstanding Language Arts teacher, came in and said, "My kids are really negative about book reports. What can I do?" I handed her a copy of my 21 ways to report on a book and she said, "Hmmm!" Two weeks later she came in with a list of 66 ways to report on a book.

When I became Curriculum Direct for the Plainfield K-12 School District, I gave this list to my Language Arts teachers. One day, Mrs. McArthur, at the Junior High School, called me and said that I really had to come to see what was happening in her 6th hour class. So I did. At the front of the room there were six students seated at a table. The leader stood up and announced, "We all have read *National Velvet*. Today we are each taking the role of one the main characters. We have come home today on Thanksgiving Day, 10 years after the end of the story in the book. We are going to have a conversation about what we have been doing during those years." She asked each of the members to stand and introduce the character he/she was playing. They then sat down and began their conversation. I got goose bumps.

The final form for students was printed on three different colored sheets of paper – creativity abounds. Obviously, some of these ideas are out of date. Do as you choose here - eliminate the obsolete or renew them; e.g., *I've Got a Secret* becomes *Jeopardy*. And, you have a lot of room for some new ground – yes, there was a time and life before computers and we did our best to survive without them.

Also, let me repeat here Mrs. Crawford's final directions at the end of the suggestions:

These are suggestions. Choose the one that fits your book and your own talents. If you can think of a good idea or your presentation, let me know if it is not on here. Do your report as soon as possible so that they will not all fall at the end of the reporting period.

The Factors in a Book Report

Input – The Book:

1. Controlled – All students will read the same book, e.g., **Tom Sawyer**
2. Free – The book will be selected by the individual student

Output – The Student's Report:

1. Controlled - The standard Book Report Form
2. The 66 Ways to Report on a Book concept

The Options

There are four options available to us related to Input and Output.

1. We can Control the Input and Control the Output
   Everyone in class will read *Tom Sawyer* and fill out the standard book report form.

2. We can Control the Input and Free the Output
   Everyone in class will read *Tom Sawyer* and use the 66 Ways to Report on a Book concept in reporting on that book.

3. We can Free the Input and Control the Output
   Everyone may choose the book they wish to read and will fill out the standard book report form.

4. We can Free the Input and Free the Output
   Everyone in class will read a self-selected book and use the 66 Ways to Report on a Book concept in reporting on that book.

Note that you will find little creativity in the Control – Control option. There is room for some creative thought in the Control – Free option and in the Control – Free option. A lot of creativity can happen in the Free – Free option.

Book Reports

1. Put yourself in the place of one of the main characters and tell the story from his point of view.

2. Act as a minor character who lived at the time and describe the action as an observer.

3. Have a panel discussion about the book -- all members of the panel must have read the story.

4. Have a quiz program, using questions about the book.

5. Make a shoebox picture of one of the scenes in the book.

6. Make a crossword puzzle using clues about the story and its characters.

7. Present a play about the story - using two or more characters.

8. Present a play about the story, acting out all of the parts yourself.

9. Give a puppet show about the story.

10. Discuss the characters in the book

11. Analyze a main character in the story (you may be either the character or a psychiatrist.

12. Give a critical discussion of the book.

13. Make your own book jacket for the book.

14. Pantomime parts from the book - there must be some oral explanation with this.

15. Oral presentation, with use of dialogue from the book - people act out different parts.

16. Draw cartoons of the story and explain them.

17. Rewrite the book using pictures and putting your captions and quotes from the book.

18. Tell what you'd do if you were a certain character in the book in one of his situations.

19. Draw pictures on the board to explain actions as you discuss it.

20. Present a TV show such as Jeopardy.

21. Write a few pages from a diary as if you were one of the characters in the story.

22. Draw a map and show the journey of any of the characters.

23. Plan an advertising campaign to get people to buy your book: posters and commercials.

24. Tell your story through pictures.

25. Draw a surrealistic picture of your book and explain why your picture contains these items.

26. Turn your book into a mystery and lead up to the climax.

27. Tell about your book using background music.

28. Use sound effects to help in telling your report.

29. Bring in costumes from the times that the story takes place.

30. Bring in props that show things used by people in the times in which your story takes place.

31. Give a character's reaction, (probable) to present day situations.

32. Write a song that tells your story.

33. Write your story in poem form.

34. Tape different parts from different songs already written together so that they tell your story.

35. Be the author and tell why you wrote this story - what was your inspiration, etc.

36. Compare the situation in the story to one with which you are familiar.

37. Tel l how you would have changed things in the story if you were the author.

38. Describe your emotional reactions to the events throughout the story.

39. Act as an animal or a utensil, etc. that saw the events in the story take place.

40. Draw the illustrations for the book.

41. Present It like an old time movie, with cards with captions on them for talking.

42. If it's a Do-it-Yourself book, explain how you'd do the project.

43. Be the author explaining your book.

44. Make a complete bulletin board display about the book.

45. Show how you would make the book into a play.

46. Write a biography of one of the characters.

47. Act out several characters and give their different reactions to the main conflict.

48. Write a telephone conversation discussing the book with a friend.

49. Give your report, then pass out a test about the subject.

50. Bring in slides which show scenes from the area as where the story takes place.

51. Bring in movies that help explain setting - similar to #50.

52. Make a giant coloring book explaining the plot.

53. Make a newspaper, with your main conflict as the Headline.

54. Give a newspaper commentary on the action in the story (Huntley – Brinkley, etc.)

55. Act as the conscience of the main character.

56. Make a notebook with pictures and information on the book.

57. Make a time line showing the order that different events took place and explain main ones.

58. Make a collage showing the different parts of the book. Explain, orally or written.

59. One person narrates - another one or more act out in pantomime while he does so.

60. Imagine a time machine and go back to the time of the story-- a "You Were There" type of approach.

61. Make a TV out of a box and then get inside and tell your story "on TV."

62. Make a train or boat out of cardboard and chug across the room until you get to your story setting and describe it.

63. If the story has a definite moral write a poem or story to point this out clearly.

64. Make a doll with a costume on it that would have been worn in those times.

65. Have a radio play - no actions.

66. Make an animated scene.

These are suggestions. Choose the one that fits your book and your own talents. If you can think of a good idea for your presentation, let me know if it is not on here. Do your report as soon as possible so that they will not all fall at the end of the reporting period.

—Mrs. Crawford

Phonics Rules and Structural Analysis

There has been some interest and concerns about phonics and phonics rules expressed in some organizations I have recently been involved with. So, I went into my archives and resurrected my course materials on the topic and upgraded them. This work is not meant to try to encourage you to use phonics or to dissuade you from its use in your work with children. It is meant to have you knowledgeable about phonics so that you can use it constructively.

Our two primary goals are Comprehension in Reading and Correct Spelling. When we encounter misspelled words, we tend to question the intelligence of the writer and the validity of the message. A presidential candidate once got into trouble by not knowing the correct spelling of a common word. (See Addendum VII)

We also must include Structural Analysis – how the order of vowels and consonants affect pronunciation, especially with words of more than one syllable. Then, just for the fun of it, let's look at some oddities in our words in the Addenda.

Phonics "Rules"

$2 + 3 = 3 + 2$ (The Commutative Property in Addition)
This "property" is a **rule** ($a + b = b + a$). A rule is correct 100% of the time.

I have some concern about labelling the phonics concepts "Rules" but since that is the term being used let's stick with it. There are a few phonics rules that hold 100% of the time, such as words beginning with gh, the h is always silent (ghost, gherkin, ghetto, ghastly) – words ending in mb, the b is always silent (plumb, tomb, comb) – but much of the time we are explaining to our kids that words such as weird are *weird* – (the "rule" is i before e except after c).

Our language is basically English but many of our words come from Romance languages, especially French, Spanish, and Italian, others have Germanic bases. Others come from wherever we may travel and eat their food so that a wok becomes a utensil in our kitchen and "wok" becomes a word in our vocabulary.

Another concern I have is that we spend a lot of time with children dealing with symbols that have no meaning of their own. The smallest meaning unit is the word. A letter by itself (other than I) has no meaning. The letter d has no meaning – if you sound it out you must attach a schwa sound to it so that it sounds like "duh."

While you are working with children, I suggest two guidelines:

1. If the word in question is phonetically sound, use your knowledge of phonics to help the child deal with that word.

2. If the word is not phonetically sound, simply accept it as a sight word and tell the child what the word is.

Let's say that the child encounters the word "game" in a story. Use whatever skills you need to use, phonics and context, to have her achieve comprehension. If the word is "sign", don't bother with a hopeless, phonetic solution; the 'g' is silent and the 'i' has no reason to be long. Just pronounce the word and go on to using context for comprehension.

Visual Learners and Auditory Learners

People tend to be either visual learners or auditory learners. Visual learners learn best by what they see and what they read – Auditory learners learn best by what they hear and the words they recall. Kinesthetic and Tactile senses are also involved. (Addendum II.)

Sight reading is a visual-based instruction. It has the children read words by recognizing the shape of the entire word. The word is the smallest unit of meaning. The word cat is recognized by its shape and by its meaning in the sentence (context). It emphasizes reading for meaning and finding the meaning of the word in the context of the sentence or passage.

Phonetic reading is an auditory-based instruction. It has children learn to read by learning the sounds of the letters and them combining those sounds into complete words. They also break unfamiliar words down into separate letter sounds and then join those parts together to form words. The most important task for children is learning the sound of each letter or combination of letters. The word 'cat' is arrived at by the combining of the sounds of the separate letters c, a, and t. Children are encourage to "sound out" the words they don't know.

Commentary #1 - The Three Basic Problems

The English language has three problems that do not exist or are much less present in other languages – the Hawaiian language is one of the best examples; each letter has a single, unique sound; each sound is generated by a unique letter or combination of letters; and each letter is sounded. **These three problems cause concerns in both reading and spelling.**

1. A single letter or blend can have more than one sound as with g: gas – gem and c: city – case. The ow combination can have two different sounds as in how and slow. The letter y can be both a consonant and a vowel as in yes and fly.

2. The same sound can be generated by different letters or blends as with the f sound in fast, phone, and laugh and the long a sound in rain, rein, and reign.

3. There are silent letters - many words have letters included in the written form that are silent in the spoken word; sign, comb, light, receipt, solder. There are no guidelines dealing with specific letters being silent.

Vowels and Vowel Sounds

The vowels are a, e, i, o, and u; also sometimes y & w. Every syllable in every word must have a vowel sound.

When we make a vowel sound, the air flows freely through our speaking apparatus. Hold your hand on your throat and say a, e, i, o, u, ah, aw, and other vowel sounds such as long o and short a and observe how little your lips and tongue get into the action.

Note that 'rhythm' has only one vowel but has two vowel sounds and two syllables.

Long Vowel Sounds

The long vowel sounds are made by saying the name of the respective vowel; a (day), e (key), i (bite), o (note), and u (cute). The letter y sometimes replaces the letter i as in fly. The diacritical marking - ā - is called a macron.

A rule: As part of a word, a vowel is considered to have the short vowel sound unless there is a reason for it to have the long vowel sound. In the word pan, there is no reason for the a to be long. In the word pane, the silent e causes the a to become a long vowel. In the word pain, the silent i creates the same result.

Long vowel sounds are also found in open syllables, words and syllables that end with that vowel, such as no, la/bel, mo/tor.

Short Vowel Sounds

The short vowel sounds are made by each of the letters; a (pat), e (pet), i (pit), o (pot) and u (put) – some vowels have more than one sound; u (put and putt). The diacritical marking – ă – is called a breve. The letter y can sometimes replace the vowel i as in gym. All of these vowels can be represented by the schwa sound as discussed in Commentary #2.

W and Y

W is never a vowel by itself – sometimes it teams up with an a as in saw, with an e as in few, and with an o as in now.

Y can team up with an o as in toy and it can take the place of a long i as in try or as a short i as in gypsum, or as a long e as in carry. (This is a problem - some dictionaries sound the y in baby as a short i.)

Vowel Diphthongs

Two vowels will come together to form diphthongs; au, aw, eu, ew, oi, oo, ou, ow, oy, ui. In a diphthong, the vowels come together to create a single new, unique sound; foot, new, sauce, boy.

The Digraphs are ch – sh – th - wh

Rule: i before e except after c –

and when it is pronounced long a as in weigh and rein and when it is followed by r as in their and weird.

Commentary #2 - The Schwa Sound

When you look at the bottom of the pages in the higher level dictionaries, you will find all kinds of symbols attached to vowels in addition to the breve (ă) and the macron (ā) for short and long vowels. When I began teaching in the elementary grades this was a real problem; having the kids sort out all those different sounds for the same symbol.

Fortunately, another concept was put into use; the schwa sound with the interesting upside-down e symbol. By definition it is the sound of the vowel in an unstressed, unaccented syllable. It is same sound as the u in cut (or duh!).

Using a common two syllable word such as **happen**, we stress the first syllable and leave the second syllable unaccented. We could spell this word with every vowel in the unaccented second syllable and they would all sound the same; happan, happen, happin, happon, happun. If you insist on saying happ-on', you just put the accent on the second syllable.

Some of the Odd Ones

Consider the ow phoneme: blow – cow – flow - how – low – vow – mow – now – and those with two sounds; bow, row, sow.

How about the oll phoneme? roll – doll – poll – moll – boll – loll.

The oo phoneme has two sounds as in good food.

The ost phoneme features this threesome: most – lost – dost.

The one phoneme gives us done – lone – gone.

A little known fact is that there are two different th phonemes; the voiced phoneme as in the word this and the voiceless phoneme as in the word thing. Some dialects deal with this simply by replacing "this thing" with "dis ting" and "dese tings."

Consonants and Consonant Sounds

All of the other letters are consonants. W and y are also consonants as in wish and yet. Make some consonant sounds; e.g., may, to, be, sue, pea; and observe how your tongue and lips are involved.

The letters c and g each have two basic sounds, the hard and soft sounds that are influenced by the vowel sound that follows them.

C followed by e, i, or y usually has the soft sound of s: cynic, central, cite, city.

C followed by a, o, or u usually has the hard sound of k: camp, coop, cut, cat.

Note: circle, cancel – the rule is followed and the two c's have different sounds.

G followed by e, i or y usually has the soft sound of j: gem, gym, gibe, ginger.

G followed by a, o, and u usually has the hard sound of g: gave, got, gum.

Note: garage, garbage – the first g is hard, the second is soft.

Y is a consonant in the words; yearn, you, yacht, yes. It is a vowel or vowel blend in; dry, toy, gym.

W is a consonant in the words: warn, rewind, wonder, wind. It does not have a vowel sound of its own, it serves only in blends; saw, new, cow.

When 2 or 3 consonants are joined together and retain their own sound, they are blends. Every letter is sounded: sp, st, sc, cr, br, pr, cl, pl, spr, str . . .

When a syllable ends in a consonant and has only one vowel sound, that vowel is short. Examples: fat, bread, fish, spout, luck, net . . . c/v/c

When a syllable ends in a silent e preceded by a consonant, the silent e is a signal that the vowel in front of it is long: make, gene, kite, rope, use, . . . v/c/e

When a word or syllable ends in any vowel that is the only vowel, that vowel is usually long. This is called an open syllable: pa/per, me, mo/tel, o/pen, u/nit, my.

When a word or syllable ends in any consonant, the vowel is usually short: strong, fun, get, cling/ing, un/cut, lost.

The infamous R–controlled rule. Pronouncing a long vowel sound before the sound of the letter r is tough on our speech apparatus so we make the vowel sound short or make two syllables. Listen to these as you pronounce them: hear - fire – care. These R-controlled vowel sounds are neither long nor short.

When a syllable has 2 vowels together, the first vowel is <u>often</u> long and the second is silent: pain, eat, boat, re/deem, say, grow. Diphthongs don't follow this rule as in law, few, bread, broad, taut.

This is a revision of the famous rule, "When two vowels go walking, the first does the talking" rule. Note that the word "often" is included in my statement of the rule.

Discussion:

Of the 1,000 most common words only 43% of the words actually follow the "two–vowel go walking rule," and 57% of the words do not. Of the top 2,000 most common words, the percentage following the rule is even lower – only 36% of the words follow the rule and 64% do not. Some combinations; ai, ea, and oa; have a slightly better record except when they are R-controlled.

Commentary #3 – Choir

Recently, I was sitting in church reading the bulletin and waiting for the service to begin. Suddenly, I focused on the word **choir** and I said to myself, Phonetically speaking this is really a strange word. It has five letters and only one of them, the r, is sounded correctly. It should start out with the same two sounds as in the word **choice**; instead it begins with the kw or qu consonant blend and the long i sound. It could be spelled **quire** and then it would also mean 24 sheets of paper - or it could be spelled **kwire.**

Actually, it has a certain uniqueness about the spelling and the sound so let's just accept it as a sight word. We simply won't use it in a spelling bee and we won't have the kids try to sound it out.

Rule: i before e except after c − and when it is pronounced long a as in weigh and rein and when it is followed by r as in their and weird.

Structural Analysis Rules for Two Syllable Words

There are basics rules for dividing two syllable words into their separate syllables and then determining the sounds of the vowels.

First, we have to distinguish between the two types of syllables:

Closed Syllable – A syllable that ends with a consonant, e.g., in the word mortar, the first syllable is **mor** – the vowel in a closed syllable is usually short.

Open Syllable - A syllable that ends with a vowel, e.g. in the word motor, the first syllable is **mo** – the vowel in an open syllable is usually long.

Rule 1. Divide the word before a single middle consonant. ("Before 1")

When there is only one consonant or blend, divide in front of the consonant, as in: **o/pen, si/lent, bea/con, ba/con.** The first syllable is an Open Syllable; it ends in a vowel – the vowel is long.

Rule 2. Divide the word between two middle consonants. ("Between 2")

Split words that have two middle consonants between the consonants: **hap/pen, pock/et, mar/gin, pon/der, for/get**. The first syllable is a Closed Syllable; it ends in a consonant and closes in the vowel –

therefore the vowel is short. In the word **pocket**, we have to consider consonant diphthongs as one consonant and not divide them.

Rule 3. Divide the word before the consonant before the ending -le.

When you have a word that ends in -le, divide before the consonant before the -le: **ma/ple, an/gle, rub/ble, set/tle, i/dle**. Then check on whether you have an open or closed syllable.

Compound Words.

Each word is accented and retains its original pronunciation: **moon/light, sports/car and house/boat**.

Prefixes.

The root word retains its own pronunciation; **un/happy, pre/paid, re/write**.

Suffixes:

The root word retains its own pronunciation; **farm/er, comfort/able, hope/less, care/ful**. In the word **stop/ping**, the suffix is actually -ping because this word follows the rule that when you add -ing to a word ending in a consonant, you double the consonant.

Addendum I – Spelling Issues

The Inductive, Analytic Phonics Model

The Inductive, Analytic Model is the basic concept for teaching reading using Sight Words. The inductive models go from the Specific to the General; that is, we take discrete facts and find a rule or generalization that would describe their relationship. At all times, **the word** is considered to be the main entity since this is the smallest unit that has meaning – single letters, other than capital I, do not carry meaning.

Analytic models have the children examine the forms and structures of words and find common factors. First, the children would deal with the written forms of the words they already know and use. Then we would have them note that some of their words begin with the same letter, such as mother, moon, and man. When they listen carefully to the spoken words and say them, they will be able to hear and feel the same initial sound. They then have learned the sound of the letter m.

The major learning modality in this model is Visual.

The Deductive, Synthetic Phonics Model

The Deductive, Synthetic Model is the reading model based on learning the sounds of letters and combining these sounds into words. Deductive models go from the General to the Specific; that is, from rules or generalizations to discrete facts. Children are taught the alphabet and the sounds of each of the letters. Synthetic models synthesize words; that is they take those separate letter sounds and combine them into one entity that we call a word. For example, we would have the children combine the sounds of the letters c, a, and t and say the word "cat". When they have learned the sounds of all of the letters, they will be able to pronounce words by combining those sounds.

The major learning modality in this model is Auditory.

Did I just read this?

Is mouthing the sounds all that you have to do in order to "read?"

Must there be comprehension?

Read these: teg, dape, fomb, loog, harb, amard, dund, ceptus, pread.

Did you actually read those "words"?

The Deductive, Synthetic Model would say, "Yes, you put the right sounds together."

The Inductive, Analytic Model would say, "No, you got no meaning."

The Learning Modalities – VAKT

Learning involves all of the sensory modalities; Visual, Auditory, Kinesthetic, Tactile (teachers often use the shortcut **VAKT** when they talk about these). This allows the teacher/parent to use phonetic and visual learning activities backed up by the other sensory abilities. Every one of us uses all of these modalities. However, individual people use them at different levels. Most people are Visual learners who learn primarily through their eyes. Next are the Auditory learners who learn primarily through their ears. Then there are the Kinesthetic learners who require muscle movement in the process. Finally, the Tactile learners who use touch along with the Kinesthetic sense.

We didn't forget the fifth sense, Gustatory, the sense of taste. It doesn't come into usage in learning very often.

Homographs and Heteronyms

1. Can you pronounce this word: bow?   How about lead?   How about close?

These are homographs (same writing) – they are also heteronyms (different names/pronunciation with different meaning). They cannot be pronounced until you either use them in context – bow - (I shot an arrow with my bow.) or use diacritical marking (bō). Here are some more:

tear	wound	entrance	read	primer	wind	sow
house	present	minute	use	desert	dove	putting
resume	address	refuse	sewer	contract	does	buffet
object	conflict	bass	invalid	live	row	kayak

Fill in the blanks with one of the words in that list:

When the quartet went fishing, the _____ caught a _____.

The answer is straight up from this ↑ arrow.

The T<u>ough</u> Grapheme

The ough grapheme has seven different sounds in the English language. Can you find an example of each of these in seven different words? I'll give you (1) 'tough' and (2) 'through'.

The others are:

    (3) though   (4) bough   (5) thought   (6) lough (pronounced same as loch)

The last is very interesting – (7) hiccough – this is the correct and only spelling of 'hiccup' that I grew up with.

Using Your Knowledge of Phonics

Can you pronounce this common word that has been spelled with some really different usages of phonics? **ghoti**

(Pausing while you think   -   -   -   -   -)

That's long enough – the word is a phonetic combination of legitimate sounds found in real words:

          The **gh** has the f sound as found in lau<u>gh</u>.
          The **o** has the short i sound as found in w<u>o</u>men.
          The **ti** has the sh sound as found in na<u>ti</u>on.
So put them all together just as you did with c-a-t to get cat and you get: fish

This is your Phonics Lesson for the Day

I cdnuolt blveiee taht I cluod aulaclty uesdnatnrd waht I was rdanieg. The gerat pweor of the hmuan mnid. Aoccdrnig to a rscheearch taem at Cmabrigde Uinervtisy, it deosn't mttaer in waht oredr the ltteers in a wrod aer, the olny iprmoatnt tihng is taht the frist and lsat ltteer be in the rghit pclae. The rset can be a taotl mses and you can sitll raed it wouthit a porbelm. Tihs is bcuseae the huamn mnid deos not raed ervey lteter by istlef, but the wrod as a wlohe.

Note that each word, though scrambled, retains the first and last letters. Our eyes are trained to respond to the beginning and ending letters of the word we're reading. Let's say that you are reading this at the end of the page:

The cowboy jumped on his white . . .

And the proofreader did not catch that the first word on the next page is **house** rather than **horse**. Would you continue reading and not notice the error? Actually, the faster you read and the more you carry the story line in your thoughts, the less likely it is that you would catch this. Excellent readers make poor proofreaders.

Read this carefully if you are running for President!

On June 15, 1992, Vice President Dan Quayle visited the Muñoz Rivera Elementary School in Trenton, New Jersey. He was invited to take part in a sixth grade spelling bee. He gave the word "potato" to 12-year-old student William Figueroa's who spelled it correctly on the chalkboard but the VP said, "You're close, but you left a little something off. The e on the end." William reluctantly made the "correction".

In his memoirs, Quayle reported that he had been relying on cards provided to his staff by the school, which he says included the misspelling. He wrote that he was uncomfortable with the version he gave, but did so because he decided to trust the school's written materials instead of his own judgment.

This episode haunted his political career and was repeatedly cited as proof along with a youthful appearance that he did not measure up to a presidential image. In his words, "it seemed like a **perfect** illustration of what people thought about me anyway."

A Few Observations

There are some sets of three homonyms such as to, two, and, too. We can add vain, vane, and vein. The one that catches my attention is rain, rein, and reign. Why? Because the most sound spelling for this spoken word would be **rane** and this 'word' doesn't exist in the American Heritage Dictionary on my desk.

We talked about the word bow as in "bow and arrow." How about its homonym, beau? Three vowels; a, e, and u; come together to make the long o sound. Well, in the paragraph above, ei and eig come together to make a long a sound.

Did you ever notice that when you say a word beginning with wh, such as when, the w sound actually is expressed before the h sound? Check this out by saying whether and weather.

Number Names

Some of the first words a child learns are the Number Names: one, two, three, four . . . We would hope that these words are phonetically sound. Let's see:

One   Should it rhyme with lone, done, or gone? Or should it be spelled **wun**.

Two   Why give our children a silent letter for their second number word?

Three   A little long but phonetically sound.

Four   Shouldn't this rhyme with flour? Our?

Five   Ah, that's better.

Six   This is a good word to introduce children to the letter x.

Seven   If you follow our Structural Analysis rules, it's sē/ven.

Eight   No comment needed.

Nine   Ah, this is good.

Ten   This is great!

Why didn't we do this with all the basic number names?

Now, Let's End This Section With Family Names – Pronounced and Mispronounced

There is only one rule on pronouncing your family name – you pronounce it any way you want to. My father claimed that his family was named Pierre in France and was changed to Pierro when they migrated to Italy to make it more Italian than French. It is pronounced three different ways by different family members – I have chosen to pronounce it my way and use a rebus (**P**|) when I start a new class or meet a new friend.

Addendum II – An Historical Commentary

The Loss of the American Golden Age of Education

In 1983, President Ronald Reagan commissioned Secretary of Education Terrel Bell to make a study of our schools and to focus on testing results. The study, *A Nation at Risk,* was a total misrepresentation of the state of our schools and made catastrophic claims that unless something was done – Our Nation is at Risk and our Schools are at Fault!

In 1990, Sandia Laboratories, our nation's testing laboratories, was commissioned by the federal government to evaluate those claims. Their report determined that the data had been grossly misinterpreted and that our schools had been steadily improving – our schools from the 1950s to the 1980s have been termed the Golden Age of American Education.

In 2001, the current reauthorization of the ESEA (No Child Left Behind) was named and proposed by President George W. Bush. Under No Child Left Behind, achievement tests have taken on an additional role of assessing proficiency of students. Proficiency is defined as the amount of grade-appropriate knowledge and skills a student has acquired up to the point of testing. Better teaching practices are expected to increase the amount learned in a school year, and therefore to increase achievement scores, and yield more "proficient" students than before.

Along with the federal mandates, state legislature and education department are now rating schools and teachers using the results of the standardized achievement tests.

The Original Intent of Standardized Achievement Testing

The standardized achievement testing movement when it was first introduced joined the classroom testing in giving vital information to our Teachers, the School Administration, and local Boards of Education to be used to improve the instructional and curricular elements in our classrooms. For many years it has done its job very well.

Now "The Tail is Wagging the Dog." Instead of the test evaluating what has been taught, it is taking over what is to be taught and how it is to be taught. This movement is now exceeding its purpose and power and testing must be returned to its proper place.

Notes:

Notes:

Notes:

Notes:

Notes:

Notes: